To my Granny Jo and Granny Marmone,
thank you for always watching over my son from above.

To Rob my partner in life and love.

And finally to my baby for inspiring me to write this book.

Hi my name is Jackson!

Here is my mom and here is my dad.

Happy as can be and never sad.

My mom is from the Caribbean
and my dad is from Ireland.
Two places I have never been.
I can't wait to visit one day.
I can't wait to go there and play.

Today we are going to the zoo.
I hope to see a duck or a snake
or a kangaroo.

Mom said "Look a lion family!"
They play and run naturally.

Mom, how did you know the lions were a family?
Mom said "look at the fur it's the same as can be."

But mom, my skin colour is different from our family.

Why is it not the same as can be?

Dad said "Jackson you are a beautiful mix of mommy and me. Let's get some ice cream and I'll show you what I mean."

Dad said "Mom will get chocolate and I will get vanilla ice cream. When you mix the two together...

you get a caramel colour supreme." I exclaimed just like me!

Mom said "You got the best of both of us. You're special, unique and precious."

Dad, what does unique mean?
Dad said "Let me paint you a picture or a scene.
If the mommy lion was brown and the
daddy lion was white,
the baby lion would be beige, isn't that right?"

Dad, sometimes the kids call me names
because we all don't look the same?
They say I'm mixed up, weird or not whole?
Dad said "they do that to be hurtful that's their goal"
They don't understand how special you are,
you outshine them all by far and far.

We then saw a group of elephants with large and grand movements.

Look there are some giraffes!
Dad said "Son, why do you laugh?"
Why does one not have any spots,
I think they must have gotten lost.

Dad said
"Can you think of why he has no spots?"
...Why oh why has he no dots?

Maybe his spots fell off
or maybe someone peeled them off?

Maybe one of his parents didn't have spots?
And maybe both parents had no spots?

Mom said
"Whatever the reason he is still special.
The other giraffes realised he's an angel.

Remember unique
qualities are what makes us different.
it is also what makes us brilliant."

Mom said "Let's go you've had a long day.
What did you learn at the zoo today?"

I learned that everyone is different in some way,
which makes them special, I'm happy to say.
My skin colour is different from my parents always.
My caramel skin will be the source of thanks and praise.

ABOUT THE AUTHOR

Marsha Cosman is a chartered accountant born in Winnipeg moved to Cayman Islands (where she met her husband) and now lives in Toronto, Canada with her family. She is an avid scuba diver, novice painter, recreational ballerina, ultimate party planner and lover of chocolate croissants. Marsha is of Caribbean descent married to a man of Irish descent. After the birth of her first child, she struggled to find storybooks her son could learn about his mixed heritage. She decided to write a book to fill the gap of this very important topic and hopes her book can reach children and families of all races.

Made in the USA
Middletown, DE
06 October 2018